Naughty Adult Joke Book

Dirty, Slutty, Funny Jokes that Broke the Censors

Jason S. Jones

Table of Contents

Table of Contents

Bluesource And Friends

Introduction

Chapter 1: Short Jokes and Punch Lines

Chapter 2: Long Dirty Jokes

Conclusion

Description

A little laughter goes a long way and certainly, *Naughty Adult Joke Book: Dirty, Slutty, Funny Jokes that Broke the Censors,* will take you to a great length. It is certainly one of the richest collections of naughty jokes for the adult audience. The book's chapters sort the jokes by their lengths. Of the two chapters, one is a compilation of some of the funniest short jokes, and the other is a collection of extremely hilarious long jokes, each with its unique setting.

Naughty jokes are appropriate for adults; they just require the right setting. You may not be found telling these jokes at a religious function, but at a social event with friends, the jokes in this book will be the highlight of the evening. Many people find it difficult to start a conversation, and good jokes can kickstart a lively conversation. Those who like to be the life of the party get their material from content as interesting as that presented in this book.

Ever wondered how some people can keep an audience for the entire day or the evening? While a number are naturally humorous, others get their material from books like this one. Reading jokes works like reading any other kind of literature; the more you read, the more you shape your mind to think in that direction. Therefore, if you train your mind to notice the queer and the funny in various situations, then you will do so even in other unrelated situations. Suddenly, your life and your way of thinking will become more positive.

To that end, it is hoped that this book will be the light that lights up your path because it will be creating a jolly mood on the inside, change how you perceive situations, and even change how you relate with others. You will become good at initiating conversations and a fun person that people will constantly look forward to speaking with. You will also teach others around you to initiate the change that you have just initiated. Overall, reading these jokes is certainly going to make you feel better and in control of what happens in and around you. Act now by reading this special book today and begin the movement that turns around the lives of people with humor!

Inside this book you will find:
- Age-appropriate jokes
- A vast collection of long jokes that provide context to make them relatable to the readers
- The most interesting collection of short jokes that makes them easy to read on the go

- The most well-ordered compilation of adult humor jokes
- Some of the most humorous jokes you want to tell your friends
- A list of some of the most good-natured jokes, none is trashy or disgusting
- Some of the most all-inclusive jokes that cross the boundaries of race, color, sexual orientation, religion, and, other demarcations
- Some of the most simple-worded jokes to promote understanding across the audience spectrum
- The most easy-worded jokes that promote memory, so you can tell them to your friends

Bluesource And Friends

This book is brought to you by Bluesource And Friends, a happy book publishing company.

Our motto is **"Happiness Within Pages"**

We promise to deliver amazing value to readers with our books.

We also appreciate honest book reviews from our readers.

Connect with us on our Facebook page www.facebook.com/bluesourceandfriends and stay tuned to our latest book promotions and free giveaways.

Don't forget to claim your FREE book

https://tinyurl.com/karenbrainteasers

Also check out our best seller book

https://tinyurl.com/lateralthinkingpuzzles

Introduction

Congratulations on downloading the *Naughty Adult Joke Book: Dirty, Slutty, Funny Jokes that Broke the Censors* and thank you for doing so.

It is often said that laughter is the best medicine and this book intends to provide you with lots of it. The jokes will brighten up your day, and you can use them to lighten up a conversation with a spouse or with friends. If you are too shy to tell some of the jokes aloud, you can also give the book as a gift.

Many people tend to avoid naughty jokes fearing that telling them would portray them to be lacking morals. However, any humor is good humor, and a person should not have to be viewed in another light because he or she considers some statement funny. A joke just requires the right audience and the right setting. You certainly will not tell a dirty joke in a church. Only find the right place and the right time, and you will get yourself and those around you cracking up and rolling on the floor in laughter.

To that end, the chapters in this book will tell short jokes, long jokes, and punch lines. Short jokes are those made up of one or two sentences. Ideally, a person asks a question, and his counterpart provides the funny answer given. The long jokes are in no way boring; they are jokes that provide context while still carrying you away with their humor. All these jokes are well-crafted and simply-worded to help you understand and appreciate them.

A lot of books on this subject are available on the market, thank you so much for picking this one. Without further ado, let's dive in and be entertained.

Chapter 1: Short Jokes and Punch Lines

Why did the police arrest the guitar teacher?
He fingered a minor.

Do you know the difference between your job and your wife?
In 5 years, the job will still suck.

What is hard, long, and full of semen?
A submarine

What name is given to the useless skin on a dick?
The man

Why are vegetarians so good at giving head?
They are conditioned to eating nuts.

Why did God create man with a penis?
So that the man would have one effective method to get the woman to shut up.

What was the vagina told by the penis?
Do not make me come there!

What distinguishes oral and anal sex?
Oral sex makes the day. Anal sex only weakens the hole.

What difference does your boyfriend have from a condom?
Condoms have changed; they are no longer thick and insensitive.

Why don't dogs marry?
Because they already are leading a dog's life.

Give another name for the vagina.
The package a penis comes in.

How are a woman and a bar similar?
Both have liquor at the front and poker on the back.

What distinguishes between a peeping tom and a pickpocket?
One grabs your watch, the other watches the grab.

How do you get your girl to scream during sex?
Call and describe it to her.

How different is a bonus check from a dick?

You will always have someone asking to blow the bonus.

How similar is life to a penis?
Your woman makes it hard.

What name is given to a guy who has a tiny dick?
Just-in!

What name is given to a guy who has a gigantic dick?
Phil!

What is 6.9?
Just another awesome thing destroyed by a period.

What is the name given to a person who will not fart in public?
A private tutor

What name is given to a virgin laying on a waterbed?
A cherry float

What name is given to a herd of masturbating cows?
Beef strokin' off

How is a game of bridge like sex?

When you got strong hands, having a partner is optional.

What is common in toys and boobs?
They were made specifically for kids, but the daddies took over playing with them.

What is the result of mixing birth control and LSD?
A trip devoid of kids.

What did the sanitary towel declare to the fart?
You are the wind beneath my wings.

What did O say to Q?
Your dick is sticking out.

What is common between a bag of chips and a push-up bra?
It is only on opening it that you realize it is empty halfway.

What did the hurricane tell the coconut tree?
Cling to your nuts more tightly; this is not an ordinary blowjob.

How can you embarrass an archaeologist?
Hand him a used tampon and ask him to determine the period it came from.

How different is a woman with PMS from a terrorist?
You are safer negotiating with a terrorist.

How should you circumcise a hillbilly?
Kick the sister's jaw.

Why do women get orgasms?
It's another excuse to moan.

What name is given to two jalapenos getting frisky?
Fucking hot!

Why do walruses always show up at a Tupperware party?
They are on the lookout for tight seals.

Why is a girlfriend similar to a laxative?
Both are exceedingly irritating.

What is the most important reason for gardening?
It allows you to get down and dirty with the hoes.

What does a sagging boob say to another?
If we fail to get any support, people will say we are nuts.

What's similar between a Rubik's Cube and a penis?
Playing with it more makes it harder.

How different is a zit from a Catholic priest?
To come on your face, a zit waits until you are twelve.

What is the best part about having sex with 28-year-old?
They are twenty in number.

What is the reason for Dr. Pepper coming in a bottle?
His wife is dead.

How different is a light bulb from a pregnant woman?
It is possible to unscrew the light bulb.

What name is given to a dinosaur found to be lesbian?
Lick-a-loota-puss

What does the banana say to the vibrator?
What is causing you to shake? She will eat me!

How is the Mafia similar to the pussy?
Once your tongue slips a bit, you are in deep shit.

Why is Santa Claus' sack so big?
He comes only once a year.

How different is a tire from 365 used condoms?
One is a Goodyear, the other is a great year.

What is the difference between a drug dealer and a hooker?

A hooker is able to clean her crack and place it back on the market.

How different is a golf ball and a G-spot?
Guys actually put effort into finding a golf ball.

What sign will be placed outside a brothel that is out-of-business?
We are closed, beat it.

Why is being enlisted in the military similar to a blowjob?
It feels better when you are closer to discharge.

What name is given to a man who is 99-year-old and still masturbates?
Miracle Whip

How are virgins from Afghan called?
Never bin laid on

What method do you take up to impregnate a nun?
Cross-dress the nun as an altar boy.

How does a woman unleash terror on her gynecologist?
By training to be a ventriloquist!

How should you get Tampon100 tickets?
By pulling strings.

Why do people constantly pick on crippled people?
Because they are unable to stand for themselves.

What prevents a chicken from wearing any pants?
Its pecker is on the chicken's head.

Why made the roll of toilet roll down the hill?
It wanted to get to the bottom.

What would be worse than spiders creeping on your piano?
Crabs crawling on your organ.

What species of bees are known to produce milk?
Boobies

What do you do when suddenly your girl begins to smoke?

Slow down, opt for a lubricant.

What does a woman who is already 99-year-old see in between her breasts that a 20-year old does not?
A navel

Why does the Easter Bunny hide the Easter eggs?
To keep people from finding out that he has been fucking the chickens.

What do you do to get retards from up a tree?
Wave to them.

What is different between aaaaah and oooooh?
Just about three inches.

Why are all men's great ideas devised in bed?
Because they plug themselves to a genius.

What name is given to a bookworm who got eaten by a cannibal?
Reader's Digest

Why are dwarfs laughing as they play soccer?
Their nuts are tickled by the grass.

When is it time to kick a dwarf in the crotch?
When he stands next to your lady and complements the smell of her hair.

What does a cannibal do when he has dumped his woman?
Wipe his ass.

What is common between McDonald's and Catholic priests?
They both shove their meat in 10-year-old buns.

What name do you give to a gang banger who has been placed behind bars?
Anything you want.

What makes women scratch their eyes when they wake up?
A lack of balls to scratch.

What does the penis tell the condom?
I am about to go in, cover me.

What part makes eating a vegetable so hard?
Placing her back to her wheelchair when you are done.

What makes Santa so cheerful?

He knows where to find all the naughty girls.

How will you know if a woman is too chubby to screw?
Pull down her pants, her ass will still be in them.

Do you know the 6 inches long and 2 inches wide that have women going nuts about?
A $100 bill

Heard of the man who died when he overdosed on Viagra?
Yeah, heard that his casket could not be shut.

State the 3 words that can destroy the ego of a man.
"Is it in?"

What name is given to having a cheap circumcision?
Getting a rip-off.

Do you know the reason why you shouldn't play Uno with Mexicans?
They steal all the green cards.

What do you call a situation where two men are fighting over a whore?
Tug-of-whore

Where would the poor live if the world is compared to a jacket?
The hood

Have you heard of the cannibal who made a number of businesspersons into Chili?
Yes, he probably likes seasoned professionals.

Define 72.
69 with 3 people watching.

A brown-haired woman tells her blonde cousin, "Hey you, I slept with a Brazilian last night." The blonde quickly responds exclaiming, "O my, what a slut! How many make a Brazilian?"

The Bible teaches on love. Kamasutra demonstrates how it ought to be done.

What does the elephant say to the man with no clothes?
How cute! But how do you manage to breathe with it?

What is the difference between a horny and a hungry person?
Where they place the cucumber.

What is common among noodles and girls?
They wiggle when being eaten.

What punishment is given to bigamists?
Two mothers-in-law.

Why is it impossible to hear a psychiatrist when he is using the bathroom?
Because of the silent 'p.'

I approached a Chinese chick and asked if I could have her number. She was excited about it and kept saying, "Sex! Sex! Sex! Free Sex Tonight!"

I grew excited and exclaimed, "Wow, Already?"

Her friend standing next to her said, "It's 666-3629."

What do you think is the difference between pea soup and roast beef?
Any person can roast beef.

Have you heard about the murderer killing celebrities?
Yeah, he was shooting for the stars.

Have you learned about the racist Mexican?
He is now a member of the que que que.

What do you think could be the worst thing about having a blonde date?
If you do not understand the hole in which to put it in, neither will they.

What name do you give to a man who masturbates while crying?
A tearjerker

What would you call balls on your chin?
A dick in my mouth.

Tell me, how can someone rape a camel?
A hump at a time.

What does the report say causes the death of the majority of the lesbians?
Hairballs

What would you say is the difference between a nail stylist and a hair stylist?

One does blow jobs while the other does hand jobs.

What will be the result of crossing a donkey and an onion?
A piece of ass which will make you tear up.

How did one hooker borrow money from another?
Let me have $20 until I'm on my back again.

What do you think separates poor white trash from a redneck?
A redneck can knock up his sister, and poor white trash marries her.

Why is fun with a prostitute similar to bungee jumping?
Once the rubber breaks, you're as good as dead.

What is the equivalent of 69?
I ate 1.

Sex without protection is always magical.
The father disappears as the baby appears.

Why is a woman similar to a road?
Both got manholes.

What did the toaster whisper to the bread?
I need you inside me.

Husband: I do not understand why you keep wearing bras without anything to put in them.
Wife: Don't you wear briefs?

What bird offers the best head?
The Swallow.

How do you prevent a French from coming into your party uninvited?
Set up a sign that reads, "No nudity."

If you cut your entire left side from your body, what do you think would happen?
I would be all right.

What do you think goes into the making of the Honeymoon Salad?
Lettuce without dressing.

What would you rate as worse than Captain Hook fingering you?

A rape by Jack the Ripper.

Explain the fact that Black men have larger penises compared to white men.
As kids, white men get to play with toys.

What would you say differentiates you from an egg?
Eggs get laid, I don't.

Do you know the flattest surface on which you can iron your pants?
The bottom of a white girl.

What do you think is the difference between a gynecologist and a genealogist?
A genealogist investigates your family tree, and a gynecologist peeks at the family bush.

What makes pubic hairs so curly?
To avoid pocking the eyes out.

What would you say has a bunch of small balls and tends to screw older women?
The Bingo machine.

What do you think tells apart a gynecologist and a bandleader?
A bandleader fucks the singers, and a gynecologist sucks his fingers.

Why do you think men like ladies with large boobs and tight asses?
They got large mouths and small dicks.

What would you have if you crossed a vampire and a gay midget?
A cocksucker.

Why is Adam the happiest man who ever lived?
He did not have a mother-in-law.

Have you heard of the Chinese couple who just got a retarded baby recently?
Yeah, the baby's name is Sum Ting Wong.

What do you perceive to be the difference between herpes and love?
Love does not last forever.

What do you do to raise a man from the dead?

Suck his dick until he cums back.

What is the fundamental difference between a black and a white owl?
The white owl says, "hoot hoot," the black owl answers back, "who dat, who dat."

What name do you give an IT teacher who gropes his students?
A PDF File.

How did you get the fat chick to your bed?
A piece of cake.

How would you identify a blind man in a nudist colony?
He would not be hard.

What name would you give to a nun on a wheelchair?
A mobile virgin.

What have you heard regarding the lesbian who used Viagra?
For a week, she could not get her tongue back in the mouth.

What name do you place on an Indian who got to do everything in life?

Bindar Dundat

What do a puppy and a near-sighted gynecologist have in common?
Their noses are wet.

What would you get if you crossed an engineer and a whore?
A fucking know-it-all!

What would a homeless woman use for a vibrator?
Two buzzing flies in a bottle.

What would you call a redneck that bursts into flames?
A firecracker.

What have you heard regarding the gynecologist who is blind?
He is only able to read lips.

What is the difference between hard and light?
It is easy to go to sleep with a light on!

What would you do if your dishwasher stopped working?
Spank her ass and ask her to keep working.

Why did God make orgasms?

To make happy women moan.

Why is it called a wonder bra?
Because once you take it off, you begin to wonder, "Where the tits at?"

What are the perks of dating homeless women?
You get to drop them off anywhere.

What did Bill Clinton tell Monica Lewinsky?
I said, "Lick my erection, not wreck my election."

What does one tampon say to another?
Nothing, both are stuck up bitches.

Why do almost all Asian chicks have tiny boobs?
Only A's are acceptable.

What would you call the white guy with the large dick?
Michael Jackson

What do a pizza boy and a gynecologist have in common?
They are allowed to smell but not eat it.

How similar are cowpeas and girls?

It is easy to pick the older ones.

How would you tell if your man has a large sperm count?
Having to chew before swallowing.

What is the difference between a joke and three dicks?
Your sister can't stand a joke.

Why was alcohol invented?
So fat women could also get laid.

What do condoms and women have in common?
They are in your wallet, if not on your dick.

What do farmers and pimps have in common?
Both need hoes for business to stay afloat.

What would be warm, pink, and wet?
A pig bathing in a hot tub.

Why is piss yellow and sperm white?
So you know whether you are cumming or going.

What is the name of the Chinese rapist?
Rai Ping Yu

How do you get a pool table laughing?
By tickling its balls.

How would you start eating a squirrel?
Spread its tiny legs.

What is the name of Moby Dick's dad?
Papa Boner

Have you learned about the arrest of the energizer bunny?
Yeah, heard he was charged with battery.

Why is the snowman smiling?
The snow blower is on its way.

A boy writing to Santa said, "Please give me a sister this time."
"Alright," Santa wrote back, "Only send me your mom."

What is the reason Santa is childless still?
He comes only once every year.

Have you heard about the junkie addicted to brake fluid?
Yeah, he says he can stop any time.

Why is a vagina similar to bad weather?
Once it wets, you have to go in.

After being married for 20 years, I still get to have blowjobs.
My wife finds out, and I am dead.

To keep relationships, women fake orgasms.
To maintain orgasms, men fake relationships.

The lightest thing on earth is a penis; even a thought will erase it.

Real men eat pink, not wear it.

How do you realize that diarrhea is hereditary?
When it runs in your jeans.

What name do you give to a broke Santa?
Saint Nickel-less

What do you call Santa who also lives in the South Pole?
Bi-polar

Why does Santa use the chimney to get into the house on Christmas Eve?
It soots him.

What did Santa tell his missus?
It's gonna be reindeer.

What goes, "oh oh oh?"
Santa Claus walking backward.

Why did the snowman seek a divorce?
His wife was a complete flake.

What do Christmas and Priests have in common?
Ornamental balls.

Why does Santa always land on the roof?
He loves it on top.

Chapter 2: Long Dirty Jokes

The New Pair of Boots

A young man was very proud of his latest purchase, a new pair of boots. He could not wait to show them off at his favorite hangout joint.

He had been dancing with this one girl for a few minutes when he told her, "I bet you that I can correctly guess the color of the panties you have on."

"Sure," she said, "Tell me what color they are."

He shot up and answered, "Blue!"

Perplexed, she said, "How could you tell?"

"My new shiny boots reflected them," he answered.

She came back a few minutes later with a lady and said, "Here, have my sister dance with you and tell me what color hers are."

Determined to excel, the young man took up the challenge and after dancing for a little while he began to vigorously rub his boots against the legs of his jeans. He went back to dancing. A few minutes later, he began asking the new girl some questions.

"What color are the panties you have on? I am having a hard time figuring that out."

The new girl replied, "I am not wearing any."

"Great!" he replied with a sigh of relief. "For a minute I thought my new boots had a crack."

Quit Seeing My Wife

John murmured to his buddy, "Man, I'm scared."

"I just received a letter from a guy threatening that he would break my legs if I didn't quit seeing his wife."

Resolutely, his friend replied, "Well, I guess this means that you will have to stop seeing her."

"Easier said than done."

"Are you that much into her?" the concerned friend asked.

"That ain't it," John professed.

.

.

"The guy did not sign the letter!"

My Mistress' Sweet Aroma

It once happened that a talented actor could no longer remember his lines. After searching for many years trying to get his career back on track, he arrived at a theater that was willing to give him the chance to get back on his horse.

The director cautioned him, "Take note that this is the most important part of the act, and you only have to say one line. You will perform it at the opening, and it will only require you to walk across the stage carrying a rose." Using only one finger and the thumb, hold the rose to your nose, sniff on it deeply and say this line, 'Ah, my mistress' sweet aroma.'"

The little he would have to do to make a comeback excited the actor. All day, as he waited for the play to begin in the evening, he rehearsed this special line repeatedly.

Finally, the evening came. The curtain went up, the actor walked across the stage as he had been instructed, and with only one finger, he impeccably delivered the line. "Ah, my mistress' sweet aroma."

The theater exploded; the audience was dying of laughter, and the director was breathing fire!

He cried, "You bloody fool! You have killed me!"

Bewildered, the great actor asked, "What did I do? Did I not say the line right?"

"No!" the director screamed. "You did not take the rose!"

The Homosexual Army Recruit

A pale young guy majestically walked into the Army Recruiting Office. The recruiting officer asked the young man a ton of questions which he answered correctly. The last question finally came. "Are you a homosexual?" The young man gladly confirmed that he was.

"Gay, huh?" the recruiter asked, "Are you capable of killing a man?"

"Yes, of course," retorted the aspiring militant, "although that would take me days and days."

The Wife and the Law

Every man's desire is to have a wife who is understanding, beautiful, a good cook, economical...

Unfortunately, the law says you can only marry one of them.

How Parents Make a Living

At Johnny's school, the teacher asked his class to state what their parents did for a living.

"What do your parents do, Mary?"

The little girl replied, "My mom is a nurse, and my dad is a lawyer."

"Well done Mary," the teacher exclaimed. "What do your parents do, Robert?"

Robert rose and proudly shouted, "My mom is a teacher, and my dad is a police officer."

"Nice. Very good Robert," the teacher told him. "Johnny, how about your parents?"

Johnny rose in haste and declared, "My mom's a hooker, and my dad's dead."

This remark landed Johnny at the principal's desk immediately. However, 15 minutes passed before Johnny returned.

"Did you let the principal know what you said?" the teacher asked.

"Yes, I did," Johnny replied. "He assured me that in this economy, all jobs are important. He even gave me a bar of chocolate and asked for my mom's number."

The Impotent Husband

A couple had stayed married for 20 years, but each time they had sex, the husband insisted that he wanted the lights turned off.

Having lived with the man for 20 years, the wife found this habit rather absurd. She decided in her heart that she was going to make him snap out of this foolishness. Therefore, in the middle of a wild steamy romantic session, she switched the lights on!

Looking down, she came face-to-face with a battery-powered leisure device her husband was holding. The vibrator was well disguised. It was soft, larger, and more wonderful than others on the market.

Realizing that the husband had made a fool of her, she went ballistic. "You impotent bastard! How could you lie to me all these years? Explain yourself."

The husband remained calm and looked at her straight in the eye.

"Alright, I will explain the vibrator…you explain the children."

God Created Eve for 10 Reasons

10. God feared that Adam would get lost in the Garden of Eden because he would be too proud to ask for directions.
9. God was assured that someday, Adam would require assistance getting to the TV remote. He would ask for it not so that he could watch what was on TV but so to see what else was there.
8. God knew that the time when Adam's fig leaf wore out, he wouldn't be bothered to buy himself another.
7. Being the keeper of the garden, Adam would require assistance finding his tools.
6. God was convinced that Adam would not stomach the pains of childbirth.
5. God was sure that Adam would forever forget to take the garbage out.
4. God perceived that Adam would never keep the doctor's appointment.
3. Adam needed someone to blame for anything that happened in his life, especially what was his own fault.
2. The Word declares that it is not good for a man to be lonely.
1. The topmost reason for creating Adam was that God finished creating him, stepped back, looked at him twice, and blatantly said, "I certainly can do better."

Social Security Kinda Sex

Jane and Ruth are in the middle of a conversation while enjoying some free time during their lunch break. Jane cuts in and asks, "By the way, how is your sex life these days?"

Ruth answers, "You know…the usual. The Social Security kind."

"Social Security?" Jane asks with curiosity.

"Yeah, when you can only get a little every month, enough to get you by."

The Royal Wedding

The long-awaited day of the wedding came, and Laura was excitedly getting dressed in the company of her entire family when she realized that she had forgotten to buy a pair of shoes.

The family began to panic. All of a sudden, Laura's sister remembered that she still had the pair she wore at her own wedding. She lent them to Laura.

Unfortunately, the shoes were quite small, and the bride had to bite her teeth trying to get her feet in. The day passed by, and by evening, Laura's feet were purple.

Once she and Edward shut the door behind them, the only thing on her mind was of how she was going to take the shoes off.

Not willing to miss any part of the action, the family crowded around the bedroom door waiting to hear any straining noises, groans, and the occasional stifled scream.

Their hopes were not dashed because they heard Edward say, "Oh God! That was tight."

"I told you she was a virgin," the Queen said with pride.

To their surprise, they heard the prince say, "Wow! On to the next one."

This time too, there was more groaning and straining.

Exhausted and panting, Edward exclaimed, "Jesus Christ! That one was even tighter."

The Duke was highly impressed and said, "That's my boy. Once a sailor, always a sailor."

The Extra-Large Condom

A blonde once walked into a pharmacy and inquired at the counter, "Do you carry extra-long condoms?"

"Yes, we do," the pharmacist replied. "Would you like to buy some?"

"No, I am waiting until some gentleman buys it."

Between The Wife's Legs

John raised his beer at the club and said, "Here's to living the rest of my life between my wife's legs." The entire club applauded, and he won the prize for the best toast of the evening.

He rushed home and excitedly told his wife, "Mary, I got the prize for the best toast of the night."

"What was the toast?" Mary enquired.

"I said, here's to living the rest of my life sitting beside my wife during church," John lied.

"That is so good to hear," Mary replied.

The following day, while taking a stroll, Mary ran into John's buddy, one he was known to drink with.

The man chuckled as he assured Mary that John had won the prize of the night courtesy of her.

Mary replied, "Aye, I know about that. It actually took me by surprise. You know, in the last four years, John has only gone there twice. One time, he dozed off and the other, I was forced to drag him by the ears, so he could move faster."

Condom Sizing Services

Harry realized that his condoms were running out, and a stand-up gentleman, he stopped at a drugstore on his way home to get a refill.
"What size would you like?" the gorgeous blonde pharmacist asked sweetly.
Harry admitted that he did not know his size quite well. Eager to help, the blonde led Harry into the backroom, lowered her pants and asked him to get into her. Harry was happy to oblige to this request.
"Size six!" she shouted after a few minutes. "Take it out. Now, how many condoms do you want?"
Harry was in a daze but managed to purchase a dozen. As he went home happily, he ran into Tom his buddy and couldn't wait to narrate his story.
Tom resolved to confirm this story and rushed to the drugstore to place his order. "I am afraid I do not know my size," he lamented.

The blonde, in the spirit of getting the order right, led Tom to the backroom and repeated what she had done to Harry. "Size seven!" she shouted. "Take it out now, and please state your order."

Tom pretended not to hear her, and when he was done, he told her, "I do not need any. I only came for the fitting." He quickly zipped his pants and grinning from ear to ear, walked out the drugstore.

Silly Magic

Two men are relaxing in a sauna. One says to the other, "Bet you, I can show you magic right here, right now."
"Sure, go ahead," the second guy responds.
"Alright, get on your hands and your knees and face away from me."
The second guy obediently gets on all fours.
"There goes…do you feel like you have a thumb up your ass?" the first guy asks.
"Oh yes!"
"Ha ha, there's the magic!" the first says waving his hands in the air.

The Penguin

A very horny man is walking down a street. Entering the first whore house he can find, he is quickly kicked out for only offering five dollars. He enters the second and is kicked out again.
By now, he is so horny that he feels like he is about to explode. He tries his luck at the next and with a weak voice says, "I am very horny, have got only two dollars and would really use a blowjob."

The attending guy assuredly answers, "Worry not. With five dollars, we can offer you a penguin."

"What is a penguin?" the horny man asks.

"Wait and see!"

The attendant quickly takes the five dollars and asks the horny man to follow him to a bedroom. Happy to get something out of it, the man pulls down his pants and lies in waiting. Soon enough, a prostitute walks into the room and starts giving the man the blow job of his life. At the point the man is about to ejaculate, she stops and walks out of the room.

Confused and with his pants dragging at his ankles, the man waddles behind her shouting, "What's a penguin? Hey! Please answer. What is a penguin?"

Oh My!

A guy sitting at the counter in a bar takes notice of a beautiful woman sitting at a table. After an hour of deliberating, finally mustering enough courage, he walks over to her and enquires, "Would it be okay if I sat next to you and chatted you for a minute?"

The lady responds by yelling, "No, I refuse to sleep with you!"

The entire crowd at the bar is staring at the duo now. The shy guy is completely embarrassed and creeps back to his counter seat.

A few minutes pass and the same woman walks up to him and apologizes saying that she is a journalist and was only trying to see how different people respond to embarrassment. The guy responds, screaming at the height of his voice, "$100 for sex? What are you offering?"

Two Hookers

Two hookers were driving around town with a sign attached to the top of their car written 'Two Prostitutes at $50."

A police officer took note of the sign, stopped them, and asked them to take it down or risk jail time.

At that very moment, another car drove by, with a sign that read 'Jesus Saves.'

One of the hookers asked, "Why did you not stop them?"

The police officer smiled and said, "That's different. Their sign is linked to religion."

The ladies humbly took down their sign and drove off very sad.

On the next day, the same cop was patrolling the area, and he recognized the ladies from the previous day driving around with a larger sign on top of their car. Thinking that he would get an easy bust, he drove to catch up with them but stopped in his tracks when he saw what the new sign said. It read, "Two Angels Seeking Peter for $50."

Bet Bet Bet

A young man accompanies his manager as he is walking down the docks. With every docker they meet, the manager bets with him that the young man has the ability to make love to one hundred women one by one, without resting, with the assurance that each woman will be satisfied. Betting begins, and all parties agree that they would meet up the next day. The following day, a group of 100 women is lined up at the dock. The guy moves straight to work and just as was promised, he is able to move from one woman to the next without pausing, and each report that they have been satisfied. He goes down the numbers: 1, 2, 3…49, 50, 51… and begins to slow down upon reaching 83…84…85…but he is still relentless and determined to reach his goal. The women continue to speak about how satisfied each of them is. The guy moves on to 97…98…99….and before reaching the last woman, he gets a heart attack and dies.
The manager is puzzled and bewildered saying that he does not understand how this could happen because "the guy had done it perfectly during practice earlier in the morning."

Seeing Underwear

The boy said, "I will give your 10 dollars if you can climb this flagpole."
The girl said, "Alright." (The girl climbs up the pole.)
The girl told her mom, "Mom, a boy gave me 10 dollars today for climbing the flagpole."
Her mom said, "The boy only wanted to peek at your underwear."

The Next Day…
The same boy said, "I will give you 20 dollars if you climb the flagpole as you did yesterday."
The girl said, "Sure, I will. Thank you."
The girl told her mom, "Mom, again, the boy gave me 20 dollars today when I climbed the flagpole, but I was smart today. I tricked him because I did not have any underwear on."
Mom was speechless.

Alligator at The Bar

A guy walks into the bar carrying an alligator. The reptile is large, about 10 feet long. The bartender bursts, "Hey man, you gotta take out that son of a b*tch out of my bar. It will bite my customers, and I will get sued."

The guy answers him, "Relax, this is a tame alligator. I can prove it."

The guy lifts the alligator and places it on the counter. He unzips his pants, takes out his package and places it in the mouth of the alligator. The alligator keeps cool, and all this time, its mouth is open. After a whopping 5 minutes, the guy takes the package out of the alligator's mouth, pulls up his pants and zips them. He proudly declares to the mesmerized crowd, "See, just as I said, this is a tame alligator. Anyone want to try it for yourself?"

A drunk at the corner of the bar says, "Yeah, I'd give it a shot, but I doubt I would be able to keep my mouth open that long!"

Blood

A woman and a man board the same elevator. The man asks, "What is your destination today?"

"I am on my way to donate blood."

"How much do you get when you donate?"

"Roughly 20 dollars."

"Amazing," the man says, "I am on my way to donate sperm, and I get $100 for every donation."

Angry, the woman gets off the elevator. Unfortunately, the duo meets on the same elevator, again, the next day.

"It is nice to see you again today. Where are you headed today?"

"To the sperm bank," the woman responds. Her mouth is full.

The Life of a Dick

A dick leads a miserable life. Its hair is a mess, its family is nuts, its closest neighbor is an asshole, its favorite friend is a pussy, and its owner hits it every now and then.

The Funny Password

A couple is busy trying to put in a new password to their shared computer. The husband types 'Mypenis' as the new password and the wife falls down laughing, rolling on the ground. She is hysterical because it reads, "Error. Inadequate length" on the screen.

The Entire Roll

Girl: Babe I'm wet.
Boy: Need a paper towel?
Girl: No, I need more than that.
Boy: 2 paper towels?
Girl: No babe, I need something bigger and round.
Boy: Damn! The whole roll?

The Blow Drier

My girlfriend caught me using the air dryer to blow my dick. When she asked to know what I was doing, "warming your dinner" was apparently not the proper answer.

Clogged the Drain

My wife stepped out of the shower and announced, "I just shaved my pussy, do you know what that means?"
"Hell yeah, the drain is fucking clogged again."

Dude on Steroids

My boyfriend said that if my post gets more than 400 likes, we're gonna try anal. Please don't like. The guy's on Viagra.

The Blueberry Hill

A boy walks into a class holding his shit, underwear, pants, and socks. The teacher is bewildered and says, "Where have you been?"
"On a blueberry hill," the boy responds.
Another boy walks into the class without socks and without a shirt. The baffled teacher asks again, "Where were you?"
"On the blueberry hill," the kid confirms.
Shortly after, a girl walks in. The teacher is even more amazed and asks her. "From where are you coming from? Atop the blueberry hill, I suppose?"
"No," the girl answers, "I am blueberry hill."

I Am a Man

Me: After every phrase I say, respond by saying, "I am a man."

Friend: Okay.

Me: You broke the relationship with your girlfriend off.

Friend: I am a man.

Me: You went and got drunk.

Friend: I am a man.

Me: You stopped at a bar.

Friend: I am a man.

Me: You checked out a fine girl.

Friend: I am a man.

Me: You asked her to follow you to your house, she accepted.

Friend: I am a man.

Me: In your bedroom, you two had sex.

Friend: I am a man.

Me: The next day, you both wake up and kiss tenderly.

Friend: I am a man.

Me: And then she comes clean and declares…

Friend: I am a man.

Sahara Pipeline

Three nuns die at the same time, and all proceed to heaven. St. Peter is excited to meet them at the pearly gates.
He is impressed by the exemplary lives they have led, allows each to give a woman's name, and promises that each would return to earth as that person.
The nuns begin to mention names. The first says, "Sophia Loren," and as she says that, poof, she's gone.
The second walks closer, "Madonna," and she's gone too.
"Sarah Piplini," the third nun says.

Peter does not know who that is. Perplexed, he asks, "Who's that?"
The nurse passes a newspaper clipping to him. He reads the headline and sadly tells the nun, "So sorry sister, but I think you got it all wrong. The article is talking about the Sahara Pipeline that was laid by 1400 men in just six months.

Swimming Sperms

Two sperms are swimming ahead of the others. One, exhausted already, turns to his counterpart and says, "I am so exhausted! Are we nearing there?"
The other turns back to him and says, "Are you joking, we are just past the esophagus."

Along With the Beats

Riding the bus, you suddenly realize that you need to fart. The music is so loud no one will hear. Being careful to time the farts with the beat, you release them one after another. Two songs are gone, and you are already feeling better. You are now close to your stop.
As you alight the bus, you notice that people cannot stop staring at you. That's when it dawns on you — you have been listening from your iPod.

Confession

A man well advanced in years is confessing and says to the priest, "Father, I have lived for 80 years now. I am married with four kids and 11 grandkids. Last night, I had an affair and made sweet love to two 21-year old girls, twice."

The priest replied, "My son, when did you last go into a confession?"

"I never have Father. I am Jewish."

"So, why the hell confess to me?"

"Are you joking? I gotta tell everyone!"

Multiple Twins

A man taking a census in a village went up to the main house in a farm and knocked. A woman answered the door, and after introducing himself as a census taker, the men went ahead seeking information about the number of children she had and their ages.

The woman goes, "Well, there's the twins Billy and Sally who are eighteen. There's also the twins Beth and Seth, they are sixteen, and the twins, Jenny and Penny who are fourteen…"

The man interrupts her, "Hold on! Do you mean you got twins every time?"

Remedy To Make It Grow

There once lived an intelligent boy. He was attending high school, and he was what you could now consider a nerd. That said, he was running a lab in the basement of his parents' home and one night, he walked up to his dad and said, "Dad, see what I just made."

The boy poured the liquid he was carrying into a bucket of soil, and some grass grew instantly.

The dad was quite impressed by what his son could do, and he asked his son to make something that would make a penis grow.

Not one to be turned down by a challenge, the son thought for a moment and told his dad that if he successfully made that fluid, the dad would have to get him a convertible. The dad agreed, and the deal was sealed. The next day, the son walked out of his lab and presented his dad with a vial. Early the next morning, the father walked up to him beaming with excitement. He told his son that he had something to gift him. Getting to the front yard, there was a cherry red Ferrari!

The son was overwhelmed and asked, "I only asked you to give me a convertible, right?"

"Sure," the dad replied. "Your convertible is stored away in the garage. Your mother bought the Ferrari."

Reading of Palms

Paul was trying to find his way down a crowded street during a fair when he suddenly spotted a palm reader. He stopped and went to sit at her table.

"For just fifteen dollars, I will read your love line and predict your romantic future," the old mystery woman said.

Paul was happy, and he readily agreed. The lady took a glance at the palm and said, "I see that you do not have a girlfriend."

"That's true," Paul confirmed.

"Oh my, you are exceedingly lonesome. Aren't you?"

"I am," Paul admitted shamefully. "That is so accurate. You can tell all that from reading my love line?"

"A love line? No, your calluses."

The Pet names

A man invited his friend over for dinner, and throughout the evening, he notices that his friend used endearing terms like Honey, Darling, Pumpkin, and Sweetheart in every statement he made to his wife. He was so impressed, especially because the couple had lived together for more than 50 years.

One time, while the wife was away in the kitchen, the man remarked, "It is so wonderful that in all these years, you have used sweet pet names on your wife."

His buddy leaned over and whispered, "In all truth, I forgot her name 10 years ago."

Cheated Three Times

In the middle of celebrating John and Mary's 50th wedding anniversary, the husband asks, "Mary, I always wondered…did you ever cheat on me in the course of our marriage?"

"Oh boy, why would you start a conversation like that one now? You don't want to ask questions like that…"
John cut in, "Yes, Mary. I would like to know. Please…"
"Alright. Yes, I did, three times."
"Three? When was that?"

"Well, remember at 35 years, when you were struggling to start your business, and no bank would give you a loan? Do you remember how all of a sudden the bank president himself came into our house and signed the loan papers and did not ask any question?"

"I remember Mary. That was you? I now respect you more than I ever did. I am honored that you would go to such heights for me. Now, when was the second?"

"Remember when you suffered a heart attack and needed a risky operation that no surgeon was willing to do? Dr. Debakey came over and did the surgery himself, and you haven't had another all this while?"

"Oh my! I cannot believe it dear! I am so touched that you would do something like that to save my life. I couldn't ask for a better wife. You must really love me, dear. Now, when was the third?"

The third time happened a few years ago when you wanted to be president of the golf club but couldn't get 17 votes."

John collapsed.

Hypnosis and Sex

A young wife was worried that their sex life was less than exciting, and she decided that her husband should see a therapist who ended up treating him using self-hypnosis. The wife was astounded by how quickly things improved. However, she noticed that each night before the lovemaking started, the husband dashed into the bathroom and remained there for several minutes.
This habit tortured her until she decided to follow him one night.
In the bathroom, she found him standing in front of the mirror practicing his therapeutic technique: "She isn't my wife…She isn't my wife… She isn't my wife…"

Women, Men, and Sex

Amy and John attended a marriage retreat, and in one of the sessions, the counselor asked each person to write a sentence and to include the words love and sex.
Amy wrote, "When two people who love each other passionately and respect each other deeply, like John and me, then it is morally and spiritually okay for them to engage each other in the act of sex."
John wrote, "I love sex."

Always Tell the Truth

A wife requested her husband to go buy her cigarettes at the local store. He walked down the street and found that the store had already closed. That option out the window, he walked into the bar across the street to use the vending machine. At the bar, he spotted an attractive woman and went over to speak to her. The duo had a nice time, and after a couple of beers, they ended up at the lady's apartment. They had a great time until it was 3:00 am. The man worried saying, "It is so late, my wife will kill me! Have you got any talcum powder?"

The woman looked around and found some. He rubbed it on his hands and went home.

His wife was waiting for him eagerly in the doorway, breathing fire, "Where the hell have you been?"

Taking a deep breath, the man answered, "Well, darling, it went like this. I walked to the store as you asked but found that it was already closed. I then walked to the bar across the street to use the vending machines there. Inside the bar, I saw a gorgeous chick and after a few drinks, we headed for her apartment and had sex."

"Are you kidding me? Let me see those hands!"

He held his hands out. His wife looked at them and went away in tears. "You damn liar! I knew you went bowling again!"

Emotional Needs

A husband and his wife are in the process of getting to cozy up to each other in bed. The passion is getting heated as it occasionally does. Suddenly, the wife stops and says, "I am not feeling it. Would you just hold me instead?"
"What?" her husband says.
The wife goes on to explain that he is not in tune with her emotional needs. The man realizes that nothing good will come out of this night and he might as well bear the disappointment.
The next day, he takes her shopping at a large department store. He walks her around and asks her to try on three of the most expensive outfits. The wife is overwhelmed and cannot choose. Her husband gladly asks her to carry all three. They then head to the shoe store and pick out some shoes to match the dresses, each shoe worth 200 dollars.
Next, the duo stops at a jewelry store, the wife picks out a set of dazzling diamond earrings, and the husband is happy to buy them for her. The wife is more than pleased. In her mind,

she wonders whether her man has flipped out, but this is not the time to care.

She even picks out a tennis bracelet to match. The husband is bewildered but says, "You don't even like tennis, but if you like the bracelet, we should get it."

The wife cannot hold back anymore. She starts to jump up and down excitedly because she cannot even believe what is happening. At last, she tells her husband, "I'm ready to go now, let's head on to the cashier."

The husband stops immediately and tells her, "No honey, I am not in the mood for making all these purchases right now." His wife's face is expressionless. "Just hold on to the items for a while."

The wife is now going ballistic, and as she is about to open her mouth to explode at him, he says, "You are just not aligned with my financial needs as a man."

More Magic

While vacationing with his wife in Las Vegas, a man went to see a show held by one of the most famous magicians. After an especially astounding act, the man, seated at the back shouted, "How'd you do it?"
"Sir, I could tell you, but I'd have to kill you after that," the magician answered.
The theater was silent for a minute before the man yelled back, "Alright then…come tell my wife!"

Huge Guy Tiny Girl

A huge guy and a tiny girl held their wedding. At the reception, a friend walked over to the guy and asked, "How in the world do you two have sex?"
Unperturbed, the big guy answers, "I just sit on a chair naked, she sits on top of it, and I bob her up and down."
His friend smiled and said, "Well, that does not sound bad at all."
"Yeah, it's like jerking off," the big guy said, "only that I have someone to talk to."

The Fruits of Love

A newly-wedded couple was spending their honeymoon in a log cabin built in an isolated place at the foot of the mountains. They had checked in on Saturday and in five days, hadn't been spotted outside even once. The elderly woman who owned the resort got concerned about them and asked her husband to go on and check on them.

The husband knocked on the door, and a weak voice from inside the cabin answered.

"Are you guys all right?" the old man inquired.

"Yes," the man on the inside answered, "we are surviving on the fruits of love."

"I see that," the old man responded. "However, would you please not throw the peelings out through the window? They are chocking my ducks!"

Conclusion

Thank you for making it through to the end of *Naughty Adult Joke Book: Dirty, Slutty, Funny Jokes that Broke the Censors*. Let's hope it was informative and able to provide you with all of the tools you need to achieve your goals whatever they may be.

Surely, this has been an interesting read, and you have thoroughly enjoyed yourself. You must have shared these jokes with your friends or partner and watched how their faces brightened up. You made their day!

Humor is always good when done right. It brings out the good or the admirable in a thing or an event that was otherwise dull. For example, so much humor has risen from the African American culture, racism and slavery, which makes thinking about them a little more tolerable, though they remain unacceptable. Through humor, you are also able to maximize pleasure, minimize pain, enhance well-being, and it helps you get along with others.

If a person new to you happens to be around as you crack the jokes in this book with your friends, be sure that he or she will never forget you. They will forever know you as the man or the woman with an incredible sense of humor. It is said that people may forget what you did to them but never forget how you made them feel. This, I have found to be true.

Now that you are equipped with one of the wealthiest collections of naughty, dirty, slutty, funny jokes that have broken the censors, go ahead and spread this cheer to others. Make others and yourself laugh, and you will find that life somehow becomes easier and more fun.

Finally, if you found this book useful in any way, a review on Amazon is always appreciated!

Jason S. Jones

Printed in Great Britain
by Amazon